Contents

Searching the sand

A shark watches the seafloor.

It finds a stingray in the sand.

The shark uses its wide head

to trap the stingray. Chomp!

The shark takes a bite.

All About
Sharks

Hammerhead

Sharks

by Deborah Nuzzolo

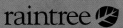

raintree

a Capstone company — publishers for children

Raintree is an imprint of Capstone Global Library Limited, a company incorporated in
England and Wales having its registered office at 264 Banbury Road, Oxford, OX2 7DY –
Registered company number: 6695582

www.raintree.co.uk
myorders@raintree.co.uk

Edited by Nikki Clapper
Designed by Kayla Rossow
Picture research by Kelly Garvin
Production by Gene Bentdahl
Originated by Capstone Library Ltd
Printed and bound in China

ISBN 978 1 4747 4309 9
21 20 19 18 17
10 9 8 7 6 5 4 3 2 1

British Library Cataloguing in Publication Data
A full catalogue record for this book is available from the British Library.

Acknowledgements
We would like to thank the following for permission to reproduce photographs: Seapics: Andre
Seale, 19, Martin Strmiska, 15; Shutterstock: City of Angeis, 13, divedog, 24, frantisekhojdusz, 1,
21, Joost van Uffelen, 5, Martin Prochazkacz, 9, Matt9122, 11, nicolasvoisin44, cover, Rich Carey,
2, Tomas Kotouc, 7, Willyam Bradberry, 23; Superstock/Norbert Probst/imageb/imageBROKER,
17. Artistic elements: Shutterstock: Apostrophe, HorenkO, Magenta10

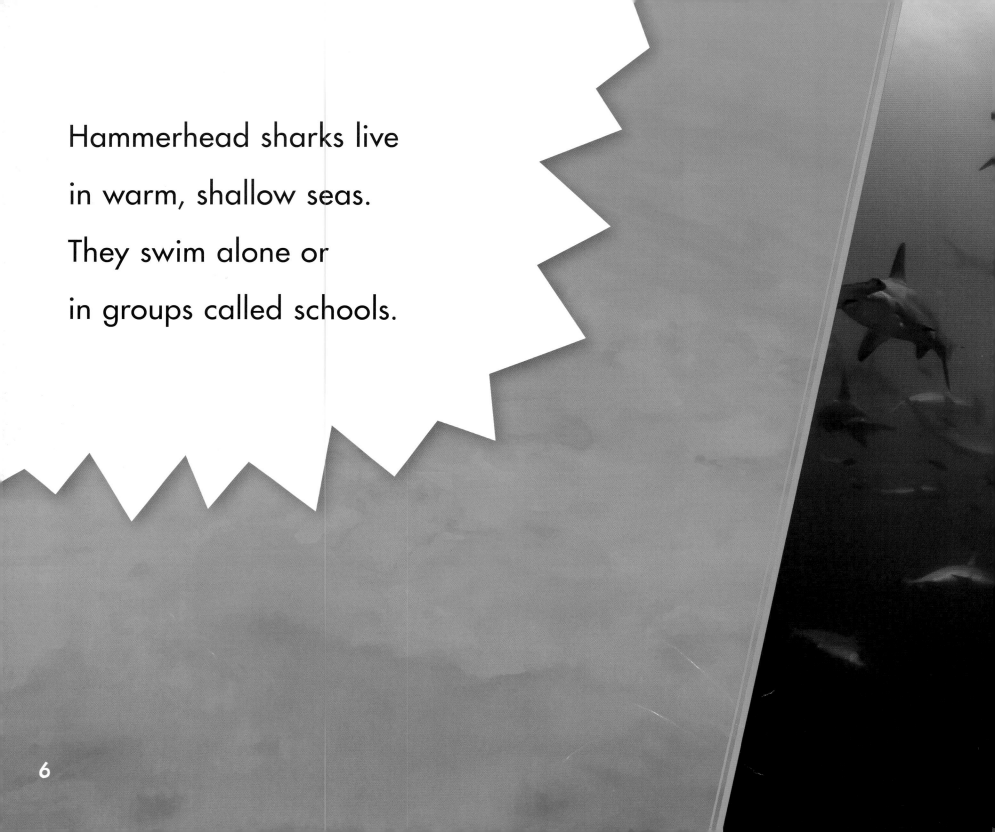

Hammerhead sharks live
in warm, shallow seas.
They swim alone or
in groups called schools.

6

A hammer for a head

A hammerhead has an eye
at each end of its head.
This shark can see
a large area more quickly
than most other sharks can.

A hammerhead shark has two dorsal fins on its back. Dorsal fins help sharks to stay balanced when they swim.

dorsal fins

Nine kinds of hammerheads swim in the sea. Bonnetheads are the smallest. Great hammerheads are the largest.

bonnethead
1.5 metres (5 feet)

great hammerhead
4.6 metres (15 feet)

1.5 metres (5 feet)

12

bonnethead

Hunting and eating

Hammerhead sharks hunt smaller fish and stingrays. They also eat crabs, squid and lobsters.

The hammerhead shark's head has special organs. These organs help the shark find nearby prey.

Hammerhead babies

Hammerhead shark pups are born live. Between 6 and 50 pups are born at one time. The pups have rounded heads.

The mother leaves her pups straight away. The pups stay together in schools at first. Hammerhead sharks live for about 20 to 30 years.

Glossary

balanced steady and not falling over

dorsal fin fin located on the back

escape get away from

hunt find and catch animals for food

organ body part that does a certain job

prey animal hunted by another animal for food

prowl move around quietly and secretly

pup young shark

school large number of the same kind of fish swimming and feeding together

shallow not deep

stingray fish that has a flat body, fins that look like wings and a long, venomous tail

Find out more

Books

DK Findout! Sharks, DK (DK Publishing, 2017)

Hammerhead vs. Bull Shark (Who Would Win?), Jerry Pallotta (Scholastic, 2015)

Hammerhead Shark (Discover Sharks), Camilla Bédoyère (QED Publishing, 2013)

Websites

www.bbc.co.uk/programmes/p02n7s0d/clips
Watch lots of amazing videos of sharks in action at this BBC website.

http://animals.nationalgeographic.com/animals/fish/hammerhead-shark/
Learn more fun facts about hammerhead sharks at this National Geographic website.

Comprehension questions

1. How do hammerhead sharks catch stingrays?
2. How are hammerhead sharks different from other sharks?
3. What do hammerhead sharks eat?

Index